THE ENCHANTED

The Enchanted

By

BARBARA MDIVANI

CHINA

BALI

VENICE

NEW YORK

Privately Printed
·1934·

·LONDON·

WHW PRESS

2016

Original edition published in a limited edition in October, 1934

and printed in Great Britain by R. Maclehose and Company Limited

The University Press Glasgow

Title page illustration by Rex Whistler

First American Edition published by WHW Press 2016

ISBN Number 978-0-9908800-1-1

INTRODUCTION BY A. ASHLEY HOFF

Woolworth heiress Barbara Hutton has achieved a kind of cult status among twentieth-century socialites. The "Poor Little Rich Girl" is remembered by many for her wealth, her extravagant lifestyle, and her desperate search for true love despite her seven unsuccessful marriages. But less known about her was the fact that Barbara Hutton was a gifted amateur poet.

Barbara began writing poems around the age of eleven, keeping journals and writing as a means of self-expression. Over time she wrote so many (her biographer Dean Jennings estimated "she wrote eighteen hundred pages of verse" by 1968) that her writing was assigned its own Louis Vuitton suitcase that accompanied her around the globe. While few of her peers really understood or appreciated her talents, a handful of friends, such as publisher Moreley Kennerly, encouraged Barbara.

"She enjoyed talking to my wife, Jean, about poetry," he recalled, "so I developed the habit of sending her whatever I thought she might like. She reciprocated by sending us samples of her work. She produced in spurts, penning reams of the stuff whenever she felt depressed or cut off from the world. It was not great or even very good poetry, but some of it was quite moving—at least it moved me.

"At first Barbara seemed rather shy about showing her work. Her poems meant a great deal to her and she labored at them. When we finally saw some of them, my wife suggested that it might give her satisfaction to have a limited number privately printed for herself and her friends. I had expected her to reject the idea totally, but as a matter of fact she was delighted by the prospect, and since I was with Faber and Faber, it was not difficult to arrange for a small edition to be produced of about two hundred copies*...On the whole Barbara was very definite about her poems, their construction and selection, and wrote without particularly wanting advice. She wrote what I would call primitive verse—unsophisticated and unschooled but full of feeling."

Barbara had her first volume of verse, entitled *The Enchanted*, self-published under the name "Barbara Mdivani" by R. Maclehose & Co., a small press unofficially affiliated with the University of Glasgow (In 1957 she published a second volume of poetry titled *The Wayfarer*). *The Enchanted* appeared shortly before her twenty-second birthday.

It was a simple, elegant book bound in Burgundy cloth with gilt edges. English artist and illustrator Rex Whistler contributed a color illustration on the title page in which he included small contrasting landscapes of New York City, Bali, China and Venice. The cover bore a gilt monogram, also apparently designed by Rex Whistler.

Dean Southern Jennings, in his 1968 biography of Barbara, wrote, "The new volume, called *The Enchanted* and privately printed in London by the Maclehose Press, contained seventy-nine of the hundreds of poems she had written. There were only fifty copies printed*—it is considered a collector's item today—and Barbara had given most of them to personal friends. Anyone interested in analysing the complex personality that was and is Barbara Hutton would find innumerable clues in this book. All the disillusionment, the self-recrimination, the

*=Various sources claim *The Enchanted* was printed in an edition of fifty, seventy-five, or two hundred copies. Whichever is the correct number, copies are exceedingly rare. *The Wayfarer* was printed in an edition of two hundred copies.

sadness and loneliness of Barbara Hutton are mirrored in *The Enchanted*—perhaps the *Disenchanted* would have been more apt—and if she ever felt tempted to produce an autobiography, which seems unlikely, she could very well say it had already been written."

Lawrence Tibbett, a leading baritone with the Metropolitan Opera, found Barbara's poetry "charming" and suggested several be set to music for him to perform at his next public recital. Encouraged by Tibbett's enthusiasm the heiress set to work, choosing the poem "In a Peking Street," which she retitled "Lantern Street (Teng Chieh)," and wrote two additional poems, "The Temple of Heaven" and "Chu-lu-mai," giving the trio the collective name *Peking Pictures*. With the assistance of Noel Coward, famed party-giver Elsa Maxwell set the three poems to music.

Tibbett premiered the songs in March 1935 on the *Packard Motors Radio Hour* while sheet-music publisher G. Schirmer, Inc., released two thousand copies of *Peking Pictures*. Only a few hundred copies were sold, earning Barbara royalties totaling $125.50. On another occasion she earned $25 for allowing scholar John Goette to include her poem "Bowl of Jade" from *The Enchanted* on the dedication page of his book, *History of Chinese Jade*.

The irony, of course, was that Barbara Hutton had inherited a $42,000,000 fortune, making her one of the richest women in the world at that time. Yet her $150.50 earnings must have filled her with some small sense of pride and accomplishment, since this was almost the only money she ever personally earned in her lifetime, and she was being paid for her abilities as a poet.

Because of the scarcity of copies of *The Enchanted* and *The Wayfarer* Barbara's skills as a writer have gone largely unseen and unknown; in fact, with the exception of excerpts from a few of the verses reproduced in biographies such as C. David Heymann's *Poor Little Rich Girl: The Life and Legend of Barbara Hutton* they have remained hidden for more than eight decades.

This then marks the first time Barbara Woolworth Hutton's poetry is being widely distributed and as a result the first time her talents have a real audience. We sincerely hope you enjoy these poems.

A. Ashley Hoff

Los Angeles

CONTENTS

JADE	PAGE 13
TUNIS	15
REMORSE	16
DETAILS	17
BEREFT	18
SUNSET	19
INCREDULITY	20
COLOUR OF GLASS	21
LAMENT OF MOHAMMED-ALI	22
ETUDE	23
ENTREATY	24
KISMET	25
LEST YOU FORGET	26
EXPECTATIONS	28
REFLECTIONS OF A COURT LADY	29
LANTERNS OF AMBER	30
JADE LOVER	31
BRIDGE BY THE PLUM TREES	32

POEMS FROM THE CHINESE

SERENELY ON THE TURQUOISE LAKE   PAGE 33

A PERSIMMON TREE   34

MY LADY LEANS UPON THE CASEMENT   35

LANG WU CASTS HIS PURPLE NETS   36

BETWEEN TOMORROW   37

MAUVE SEA SONG PAGE   38

HARVEST OF DREAMS   40

ARAB SERENADE   41

ARAB LOVE   42

SONG OF SCENT   43

ENIGMA   44

MIRAGE   45

GRAND CANAL: MORNING   46

THE LIDO: AFTERNOON   47

PIAZZA SAN MARCO: EVENING   49

GONDOLA RIDE: NIGHT   50

TO A PROFESSOR   51

DESTINY   52

DISCORDANCE   53

METEOR   54

UNPREMEDITATED	PAGE 55
YESTERDAY'S DUSK	56
I HAD DREAMT—	57
ENIGMA	58
PARTING	59
INTRUSION	60
BOWL OF JADE	61
AFTER	62
SILENCE	63
REQUIEM	64
IN A CITY	66
ILLUSION	67
WILL YOU REMEMBER?	68
TIME TO GO PAGE	69
SOLACE	70
RED ROSES ON A BOAT	71
BROKEN INTERLUDE	72
SEA BLUE	73
BROKEN DREAMING	74
HONOLULU	75
ROME	76

DUSK IN BALI   PAGE 77

STAR DUST   79

ROAD TO FEZ   80

THE ENCHANTED   81

RAVELLO   82

NAPLES FROM PAOLO'S HOUSE   84

TO VENICE   86

MOONLIGHT IN GRANADA   87

TREES   88

SUNSET AT THE SUMMER PALACE   90

IN A PEKING STREET   91

RENCONTRE   93

PRAYER FOR LIGHT   95

LAST NIGHT   96

TO —   97

PATTERNS   98

A PLAINT   99

THIS SPRING IN PARIS   100

A SHADOW   101

ADIEU   102

JADE

O WORLD, I love you
For having made
A thing of beauty
As rare as Jade:

That holds within
Its polished sheen
The hue of hills
Alive with green;

That breathes the still
Fragrance of rain,
Falling coolly
Upon a plain;

That recalls the
Clear look of streams,
Bubbling through woods,
Like crystal dreams;

That speaks the fresh
Laughter of spring,
In meadows where
The skylarks sing;

That calms the ache
Of hungry hearts
With silence that
Its green imparts;

That fills the eye
With radiance
Of evening skies
Upon a glance;

That tells of pure
And noble ways,
To lighten all
Our lonely days;

That cools the brow
Like touch of snow,
Till all our petty
Troubles go;

That music tells
Of green-waved seas,
To flood our lives
With melodies.

O World, I love you
For having made
The whole of heaven
In a piece of Jade.

January 13th, 1934

TUNIS

In shining beauty
Mosques arise,
Cloud-enshrouded,
Toward the skies,

With domes of jewelled
And passionate white,
Like breasts of dancing
Girls at night.

While with dusk
The stars awake
As silver lilies
In a purple lake.

1930

REMORSE

Is there forgiveness, think you,
For casting love aside,
For lack of courage,
And for false and foolish pride?

Is there forgiveness for
Killing the only thing
That made your life a garden
Filled with birds that sing?

When love is gone, what else remains,
What else, ah me, indeed;
Except an aching loneliness,
And a bitter aching need?

No more is laughter in the sun;
No more is music sweet;
There is nothing but an empty void
Where once our eyes did meet.

Pray, is it worth the sorrow,
This taking of your life;
When love is dead and vanished
What else is worth the strife?

Perhaps there is forgiveness
When you have known regret,
Bur surely you could never
A single hour forget.

May, 1931

DETAILS

THE little things that pass unnoticed
Furtively,
Have become of great significance
To me.

The grace of hands whose fingers tremble
Suddenly;
Hair that a second holds the sun
Triumphantly;

And eyes that by a glance may sing
A rapture;
Or mouths that curve of dreams a man
May capture.

O little things that pass unnoticed
Stealthily,
Have become the breath of life
To me.

May, 1931

17

BEREFT

I AM utterly bereft,
Nothing now is left;
Only a thought of you
This emptiness to woo.

I am like a barren beach
Beyond the sky's reach;
Merely a silent sky
That saw the sunlight die.

May, 1931

SUNSET

The sinking sun made a little
Glow on the sand,
And the ocean covered it
With one white hand.

It was iridescent gold
Trembling with light;
One small second of glory,
And then came the night.

July, 1931

INCREDULITY

ASSUREDLY, it is hard to believe That I should grieve
Over you,
In the helpless manner
That I do.

Nor could I reason why
This grief of mine
Is past reply.

Think you that my tears atone
For having left you
All alone?

July, 1931

COLOUR OF GLASS

GLASS-coloured body
Fashioned of stars
Hammered with star-dust,
Scented of flowers.

Beautiful body
Exquisitely moulded
Of glass-coloured water,
Star enfolded.

Dream drowned body
Limpid with light,
Lain among roses
Crimson and white.

Crystal clear body
With moon-woven hair,
Folded in music
Colour of air.

July, 1931

LAMENT OF MOHAMMED-ALI

LITTLE feet burdened with love,
  Weary from endless waking;
I have kissed the road you tread,
  Bright with the sun's making.

    Under the mango tree
    I hear the bulbuls call;
    The air is soft with flowers
    Here by the palace wall.

  Your feet are bound in silver
Making sweet music where you go;
  O lovely dark-eyed maiden,
    Why should I love you so?

  The tender beauty of your face
  Has haunted my sleepless bed;
And the thought of your little feet
Goes wearily through my head.

  My mind is torn with longing
    Under the mango tree;
  O Allah, that a Hindoo girl
Should have captured the heart of me.

February, 1932

ETUDE

IT seems I could never tire
Of watching your lovely
Sensitive face,
Where the lights come and god
Like sunlight on roses;
The sweep of your brow,
And the tender lines
Smiling has worn
About your eyes,
At once so sombre
And star holding.

Never weary of the sadness
Shown in the suggestive
Droop of your sweet lips,
Half-mocking,
Half-pleading.

Never cease to marvel
At the beauty of line
Where throat kisses chin;
Carved as though
Of cool lilies,
And sleek as silver;
Or the delicate Perfection of your nose,
And willow-slim brows.

March, 1932

ENTREATY

HOLD out your hand
To help me across
The dark lagoon,
My friend;
Your hand is strong
And clean,
Holding easily
All of my heart
In its palm.

The lagoon is wide
Submerged in Shadows strange,
Wherein stars struggle
Frantically for breath,
Swimming madly
In silver confusion.

Would you begrudge
Me the aid
Of your hand
That carry carelessly
All of the sunsets'
Enchantment upon
Your shoulders?

July, 1932

KISMET

MY belovèd, long ago
You were my lover.
That I know.

In some forgotten Arab night
On desert sands
We pledged our plight.

Till the Eastern stars hung low,
We knew of love
All one may know.

For one mad enchanted time
That grace of yours
Was wholly mine.

Perhaps you were a Pasha's son,
And I the maid
Your sword had won.

Yet, might it not again be true
When each lonely night
I long for you?

July 11th, 1932

LEST YOU FORGET

LEST you forget
My love for you,
I will set it high
In the sky of blue,

To cover your head
Asleep or waking;
It will fall as dew
When day is breaking.

Lest you forget
When I am gone,
My thoughts of you
Like clouds are born
To blow about
Your haughty head,
Recalling dreams
Of words we said.

Lest you forget
The pain of parting,
It becomes an arc
Of rainbow starting,

From highest-heaven
To far-flung hell,
In a way you should
Remember well.

Lest you forget
My tender care,
I will spread its
Fragrance in the air,

Clinging to every
Blossom or tree,
Recalling to you
The presence of me.

Lest you forget
My love was lovely,
As a throbbing song
In skies above me,

I made it a moon
Of pale delight,
To enchant your eyes
With my love each night.

1932

EXPECTATIONS

I must sing a song of ecstasy,
They expect it of me;
And I must laugh,
To fill the world with glee,
They expect it of me.

A thousand joyous things
I must do,
They expect me to.

Well, the devil take them
And their expectations,
All they will get from me
Is lamentations.

1932

REFLECTIONS OF A COURT LADY

LANGUIDLY I lean over
Jade Girdle Bridge
At twilight,
Like a slender lily stem
In my peach-coloured gown,
In idle contemplation
Of the shadows that fall
On the turquoise water.

Also not displeasing
Is the reflection
Of my face therein;
The surprising beauty
Of my long dark eyes
Set like enchantment
In the moonlight
Of my silken skin,
Is delightful.

I smile while noting
The jewelled butterflies
On my headdress
Dancing lightly in
The musical sunlight.

January, 1933

LANTERNS OF AMBER

YOUR eyes are lanterns
Of Chinese amber
Hung within the high
Hollows of my heart,
Curved like crescent moons
To my broken dreaming.

I am pale and lost with anguish
From looking on them night and day;
Will you not in mercy remove
From my vision
The incessant beauty
Of such sweet
Amber indifference?

January 9th, 1933

JADE LOVER

LOVELY jade body of my lover,
Coolly clear as an amber flower,
I have laid you on my bamboo bed
For a last light rest in this unblest hour.

Your long dark eyes have hurt my heart
With muted music that dead men make,
And the grace so tragic of your hands
Lying like swans on the sombre lake.

Of your stately robe of dark plum hue,
Has broken my humble heart in two.

January, 1933

BRIDGE BY THE PLUM TREES

IN my ceremonious gown
With beads of amber and peacock plume,
Eagerly I await your presence
Beside the bridge where the plum trees bloom.

On this auspicious day my eyes
Are quick to note your slow approach,
As hesitantly, in swaying silks,
Your timid steps my fears reproach.

With downcast glance and ivory cheek,
Like a shaken song of purest jade,
You gravely hear my courteous speech,
Refusing not the poems I have made.

We converse until the shadows fall
Like faded flowers upon your hair;
Then part reluctantly when first
The painted moon climbs her star-strewn hair.

January, 1933

POEMS FROM THE CHINESE

I

SERENELY, on the turquoise lake
    We balance our lily boat;
    You, with one jade-slim finger,
    I, with the longing in my eyes.

POEMS FROM THE CHINESE

II

A PERSIMMON tree
Grows in my garden,
O wiser-than-jade
Lee Wang Fei;
Each moon I await
Your perfumed presence
Beneath the boughs.

POEMS FROM THE CHINESE

III

MY lady leans upon the casement
In the beauty of her long-sleeved gown,
Her heart is like a river flower,
I, the worthless stone that weighs it down.

POEMS FROM THE CHINESE

IV

LANG WU casts his purple nets
Within a jade-green sea;
Hopes he to ensnare a Precious Pearl,
Or a few forgotten dreams
Of an Emperor?

January, 1933

BETWEEN TOMORROW

YOU stand between me and the deep-voiced aching
    Of silence eternally stilled in my throat;
    Between me and the dread of thin music
    Insidiously star sung, in wavering note.

    Between me and the searing caresses
    Of sunsets, gem hung on a bronze beaten sky;
    You stand like Beauty incarnate, remotely
Between me and wan thoughts of passion passed by.

    Like laughter of wine, agèd and mellow,
Long weaned from the breast of brown savage earth,
    You stand between me and the sorrow
    Of orchard boughs bended with dearth.

    You stand between me and the mockery of
    Life, tossed as a husk to the Godhead of pain;
    Between me and the arid wisdom of dying,
    You stand like a lovely promise of rain.

February 28th, 1933

MAUVE SEA SONG

DEEP, deep down in a lilac sea
I gaze with anguished eyes,
Where stars are fallen in great bouquets
From the scornful brilliant skies.

'Tell me, O Sea, have you seen my Love,
Have you seen my Lovely One?
His hair is gold as the autumn moon,
His eyes more clear than sun.'

He left me to sail in a silver barge
To the heart of the lilac sea,
To quest of a gem hard hidden there
To lay at the feet of me.

When sunset had flung a scarlet scarf
Across the western sky,
I watched him fade in the flaming light,
And my eyes were glad and dry.

But he never returned in his silver barge
For the heart of the lilac sea;
That is the reason I wander here
So inconsolably.

'Tell me, O Sea, have you seen my Love,
Have you seen my Lovely Dear?
His mouth was music of curved delight,
And his voice was rich and clear.'

But never an answer the mauve sea makes,
  Never a murmured sigh,
And the fallen stars stay cradled deep,
  Deep down where the corals lie.

May 8th, 1933

HARVEST OF DREAMS

GO gathering dreams, my soul,
Unremembered in the dusk,
Bind their bruises with one white hand,
Anoint their feet with musk.

Capture their fragile bodies
In silken robes of soft delight,
Fashioned of bird song at dawning,
And green star song at night.

Build for their shaken beauty
A palace of woven air,
Where roses lie red for their resting,
And moonlight falls sweet for a stair.

Then when, my soul, you have garnered,
This harvest of ecstasy,
Go gathering dreams that are tarnished,
To fashion a crown for me.

May 8th, 1933

ARAB SERENADE

TO-NIGHT the clouds like camels lie
    Huddled close against the moon,
  The stars are groups of Arab tents,
    And the wind a plaintive tune.

  Across the desert sands he comes
    On a stallion shod with fire,
  And the arid heat of the savage night
    Is scented with strange desire.

I have bound my hair with jasmine flowers,
    And my hands are laden with gems,
  My fingers are dyed with henna, bright
    As the reddest of coral stems.

'Come, gather me swift in thine arms, my Lord,
    Let me swoon at the sound of thy voice;
  Let me rest this hungry glance on thee
    And in the light of thy beauty rejoice.

  'The hour grows dark and I seem to faint,
    So great is this longing for thee;
  O hasten to join me where I stand
    Beneath the boughs of a banyan tree.'

  How well I recall the touch of his lips
    And the sombre fire of his eyes;
  In mercy, O Stars, light the way of my
    Lord, with the light of a million skies.

May 9th, 1933

41

ARAB LOVE

A HOST of old desires rise
And reel about my head in taunting grief;
'Come, bend your honeyed mouth to mine—
The hour is ours, and I would be brief.'

Each lobe of her ear is laden
With gems that flare like flames in the night;
'O lend me your soul to ease this ache;
Mine is all dark, and yours so light.'

Her eyes hold rivers of drowning stars
That moisten my pale and fevered brow;
'Your breasts are cool roses beneath my touch;
Lie close on my heart—I would love you now.'

Still a host of old desires
Swell and sweep like ghouls before the moon;
'The dawn draws near, depart in peace;
I have wearied of love too soon.'

May 9th, 1933

SONG OF SCENT

THERE is a perfume about your presence
    Cloying with myrrh of words unsaid,
    A subtle fragrance in each movement,
That makes the blood beat in my head.

With every glance, and every gesture,
    Of darkening eyes and flame-white hand
    Laid lilting light upon my shoulder,
My senses surge through scented land

To where the trees are stark with beauty
    Beneath the burdened twilight skies;
Where your mouth is melted golden laughter,
    And the night your hair across my eyes.

There lies a music about your body
    Reminiscent of harp-wrung Greece,
    A minor prelude in roseate curves,
That makes my pulses sob and cease.

I reach to hold, I strain to clasp
The moon-drenched song of your slender feet,
    That flash from star to eager star
Through bewildering haze of summer heat.

To where the wind is wafted far
    From blue burned days of salted seas;
To where your breasts rise hills at dusk,
    Sweet with flowering melodies.

May, 1933

ENIGMA

WHITHER go the thoughts
When glances meet,
Like sword to sword,
Across the street?

Do they take flight
Like frightened birds,
Into the void
Bereft of words?

Whither go the dreams
When hand finds hand,
Under the night
By silver spanned?

Do they seek peace
By surging seas,
Wreathing their brows
With melodies?

And when the pain
Of heart on heart,
Becomes so great
No words in part

Can soothe the need
Or ease the ache;
Whither go the schemes
That mortals make?

May 9th, 1933

MIRAGE

WANDERING under a spacious dome of sky,
Where rain in laughter prosecutes the dry
Of empty days and vacant night,
I stop to ponder on the plight
Of man's passage far beyond the void
Of this ancient world, undestroyed
By thoughts arising behind the brain,
Or the deep significance of pain
Lingering quiet where astonishment lies,
In touch of hand, in glance of eyes.

Dimly I conceive the graying end
Of eternities, that relentlessly send
Us vainly to grope like ghosts in the dark;
Poor faltering mists that shroud the stark
Reality of life with camouflage,
Until it seems a dream, a nebulous mirage.

May 10*th*, 1933

GRAND CANAL: MORNING

THE water burns pure
Like azure flame
Beneath the morning sun
With scarcely a breeze to tame
Or abate its ardour;
And the sky overhead
Seems smouldering
Like molten lead.

On either hand
Rose palaces rise
Like drowsy mermaids,
With tender eyes;
And from their hair
Confusion of flowers
Fall over balconies
In coloured showers.

Through marble casements
Glimpses are caught
Of yellow roses
In green vases, wrought
With masterly craft;
And often a sweet song
From across the waters
To my heart is borne.

May 11th, 1933

46

THE LIDO: AFTERNOON

FROM where I lie
Idle in the sand
That is warm with sun
To the touch of my hand,

I see orange sails
Against skies
Of piercing blue;
And closing my eyes

I feel them press
Like amber burning
Across my eye-lids,
And uneasily turning

I hide my face deep
Within and arm;
And for a while
Their penetrant charm

Is forgotten;
then all at once, I know
The sudden hurt
Of sails that slow

Press apricot souls
Hard upon my heart,
And lifting my head
With anguished glance, I start,

And cry aloud
To the heedless air,
Shaken with sobs,
And racked with despair.

O how to express
This ecstasy
Of flaming sails,
Flung over the sea

In beauty that knows
No end, no slaking,
But will always consume
Me, asleep or waking.

All my life, will I
Never be free
From the sight of these sails
In the heart of me?

May 12th, 1933

PIAZZA SAN MARCO: EVENING

SILENTLY, I watch the pigeons fly
Low under the green of an evening sky,
Or strut with steps absurdly vain
Where footprints of arrogant nobles have lain.

Raising my eyes until they lie
On a fresco of blinding colour high
Placed above San Marco's door,
In patterned mosaic, I dream before.

How Doges came in crimson dress
To pray in meek submissiveness
Within the calm and holy place,
The light of candles on each face;

And I feel my heart about to break
With the indefinable ache
Of ancient beauty, that still lies
In all its glory before my eyes.

Turning, my glance rests on your lovely face
Again, as you stand with easy grace
Beside me; and together we watch where
The dusk falls like lilacs across the square.

O World, I cry, can this be true?
Are you the same that once I knew?
Or if I dream, then let me be:
This is all I would know of eternity.

May 11th, 1933

49

GONDOLA RIDE: NIGHT

Venice stands like a masked woman
With jewelled hair, under the night;
And the water whispers caresses
About her feet of shadowed white.

Down narrow canals our gondola
Glides like a ghost with bated breath;
And only a drifting echo of laughter
Breaks a silence more subtle than death.

Beneath bridges curving like pale
Arms exquisitely overhead;
Around corners reeking with stench
Of stale waters, and things that are dead.

Beside cafés crowded with people,
Flooded with lights, and gay with song;
Close to churches that bare dark breasts
To the hungry heavens all night long.

By marble palaces laden
With flowers overpoweringly sweet;
By evil houses of ill repute,
Near mooring stairs where lovers meet.

Then out upon the Grand Canal
Where the drenching moonlight lies
Richer than silver spices,
On the water, and in our eyes.

May 12*th*, 1933

TO A PROFESSOR

HELLENIC face of tranquil beauty
Carved of marble white as snow,
With what sweet serenity
Did the Gods endow you long ago?

On that brow so eloquent
Of noble days and lofty dreaming
The art of Praxitiles
Has found a true and finer meaning.

On that cheek and in those eyes
There lies a strength of calm repose,
And great delicacy is traced
In the pure line of your perfect nose.

Harps of Apollo once sang
Lyrical lays of exquisite grace,
That live again at the sight
Of your ageing and beautiful face.

April 5th, 1934

DESTINY

IF I love you, do not blame me,
Rather blame cruel Destiny
That decreed an aeon ago
One day I would love you so.

When the flames of silver fire
She wrote my story of desire
Shamelessly across the sky
To startle angels passing by.

Moonbeams were born to love the sea,
The flowers to blossom endlessly;
The trees were made to bring you rest,
And day to die on twilight's breast.

So by all the laws divine
Were you created to be mine,
Then blame me not, for well I know
My love was born an age ago.

November 24th, 1933

DISCORDANCE

AFTER you are gone,
Leaving me alone,
How harsh the endless mutter
Of the city's undertone.

I stand as one bewildered
Before the pain of light,
And my eyes are numb with laughter
That has frozen in my sight.

Still the clamour rises
And discords rend the air,
There is madness in the medley,
And death seems everywhere.

Walking down the street
I stare from face to face,
And hunger meets my glances
Where youth has left no trace.

Deep within my heart
I hide my dream of you,
I am tortured by this bitterness
Lying naked to my view.

September 24th, 1933

METEOR

YOU have come to love me suddenly
And rather strangely too,
My heart is like a barren beach
Where the sea has surged anew.

Your love has brought me radiance
Of a green swept plain in spring;
And my thoughts have flown like eager birds
From these walls of suffering.

Your hands have told me endless tales
Of intricate loves long dead;
And your eyes have worn me thin as stars
That shine as crystal overhead.

The beauty of your voice is like
Dreams of darkening woods at night,
Where time is hung like gossamer
Between us and to-morrow's light.

Your words are clear and cool as bells
And significantly remote,
Falling on my quivering soul
As in a lake where lilies float.

November 25th, 1933

UNPREMEDITATED

I HAVE tried to love you lightly
But without success,
To love you very little
And never to excess.

I have sought to love you wisely;
But this I cannot do,
For all my vows are shattered
Each time I look at you.

November 26th, 1933

YESTERDAY'S DUSK

CAN it be but yesterday
That I was to near you,
When your voice was rich with laughter
And your eyes were coolly blue?

Where a host of buildings rose
And leant against the skies
Gem-hung like Arab palaces
That in a dream arise.

Can it be but yesterday
I held you in my heart,
Or is it then a thousand years
That we have been apart?

November 26th, 1933

I HAD DREAMT—

I HAD dreamt your love would be
A simple lovely thing,
Unfruaght by savage words
That lead to suffering.

I had dreamt your love would be
As a blossom-laden May,
Fragrant for the mind to store
In melodies of yesterday.

But derision scorns my dreams,
Has turned it ashen cold and gray,
For love was dead within your heart
When leaving me today.

November 28th, 1933

ENIGMA

I HAVE carved your face for my delight,
A Mongol face of bronze and light,
With all the shades and subtle hollows
Of cheek and jaw and mouth that follows
Derisively a curve of passion
Slightly cruel in its fashion;
And eyes that wear a piercing look
Of starlight fallen in a brook,
Mongol eyes in form, though blue
And coldly clear as frozen dew,
A Western man with Mongol face;
Strange harmony of scorn and grace.

November 30th, 1933

PARTING

ACROSS the void of parting
I turn to say farewell,
Let your lingering glance be gentle,
Discreet as a silenced bell.

Let remembered words of laughter
Vanish in vacant light,
And the knowledge of love diminish
Before the depth of night.

Across the void of parting
I turn to say farewell,
And my heart is like a captive bird
Caught in a prison cell.

November 30th, 1933

INTRUSION

EACH night when I return
Wearily to my room,
I seem to feel you standing
Close beside me in the gloom.

Glances your eyes once gave me,
Some words that you let fall,
Have painted brilliant pictures
That illuminate my wall.

The bed of yellow satin,
Green cushions on the chair
Are laden with your fragrance
Pervading in the air.

O, will you not begone,
And cease to torture me?
Your love is but a farce
Wherein you alone are free.

December 1st, 1933

BOWL OF JADE

I bring you a bowl of jade
For your slender hands to hold,
Green as the mountain waters,
And infinitely old.

I pray you to place it gently
On a table of gold brocade,
Like an emerald glowing
In either sun or shade.

Then you should strike it softly,
The music that you will hear
Will be as clear as bells of heaven
Ringing in your ear.

The texture is smooth as petals
And cool beneath your touch;
It will soothe away all sorrow
Should you caress it much.

I bring you my poor dreams
Caught in a green jade bowl,
Carved untold years ago
Out of a Chinese soul.

December 18th, 1933

AFTER

SHOULD the sea lose the light of stars
To lie desolate and dim,
So will the temple of my heart
Be darkened when leaving him.

Should the hills be shorn of flowers
They hold softly to their breast,
And the sunlight sink forever
In the flame-enchanted West;

Should the birds forget their singing
Where the plains stretch stark and drear,
Will the summer of my heart
Lie broken without him near.

December 20th, 1933

SILENCE

ALWAYS when with you
The words I long to say
Tremble in my heart
Till you have gone away.

I dare not speak aloud
For fear perchance you might,
Knowing once their beauty,
Flee from me in fright.

So close within my heart
They rest like butterflies,
All speech with you is held
In glances from my eyes.

Yet may I not one day
Reveal to you my heart
With words as sweet as song
Before the time to part?

December 23rd, 1933

REQUIEM

O BEAUTY, I would hold you
Hard upon my heart,
So that to my loneliness
You may impart
Your loveliness.

I would blind my eyes
With coloured ecstasies
Of brilliant skies
Above burnished seas,

So that never to my mind
May return again
His face so well defined
To taunt my bruisèd brain.

I would numb my hearing
With wild melodies,
So his voice endearing
May not recapture these

Poor moments of liberty,
That since leaving
You have granted me,
Tenderly relieving.

The weight of wanting
That stifled my being,
By brightly flaunting
Your grace for my seeing.

O Beauty, I would hold you
Hard upon my heart,
So that to my lovelessness
You may impart
Your loveliness.

December 24th, 1933

IN A CITY

ONLY five streets divide me
From him whom I love,
Yet they seem the infinite
Space of sea and sky above.

For he can never know
At night if I should weep
Or hear if once I called his name
Aloud within my sleep.

I sit disconsolate
Within my lonely room,
And my thoughts like shadows flee
Toward him through the gloom.

Only five streets between us
Seems but a little thing
To cause such waste of happiness,
Such wealth of suffering.

December 28th, 1933

ILLUSION

BELOVÈD, why do you haunt
My restless sleep,
With tender words
You never speak?
It only makes awaking
More poignantly heart-breaking.

A barren hill
May dream of rain,
And the sweetness
Coming after pain;

A starless sky
May dream of dawn,
Where grasses green
The ground adorn.

Yet how I dare
Have dreams of you
That never could
In life come true?
It only makes reality
For me a greater tragedy.

December 29th, 1933

WILL YOU REMEMBER?

Will you remember when day
Has died upon my leaving,
Will you stay in loneliness
And silent grieving?

Will you remember words that
Smiling I would say,
Dreaming how I used to look
Before I went away?

Will you remember seeking
To clearly understand
The reason why you held my
Heart within your careless hand?

Or will you with a gesture
Then dismiss me from your mind,
Forgetting all the happiness
That now I leave behind?

December 30th, 1933

TIME TO GO

IT is the time to go.
I feel the train's slow
And ponderous wheels start
Heavily across my heart.

I hear the engine's shrill
Cry of parting, and still
I speak words of easy grace
And smile from face to face.

Knowing in a little while
Each lean and hungry mile
Will take me far away
From where I long to stay.

January 4th, 1934

SOLACE

I SEE my belovèd everywhere,
For he is in my heart;
Though distance may divide us
We are not apart.

For when I walk with other men
And look upon their grace,
I only see the loveliness of
His familiar face.

Or when I speak with other men
Hearing words they say
the music of his vibrant voice
Will drive their words away.

No matter where on earth I go
the knowledge of him near,
Will shelter me from loneliness
And calm each foolish fear.

January 5th, 1934

70

RED ROSES ON A BOAT

ROSES red as silken rubies
Before a wall of green,
Lovelier to my weary sight
Than aught in life I've seen.

Roses swaying in crimson grace
Like silken butterflies,
Against a wall of softest green
Breathe music to my eyes.

With every rise and fall of waves
They bow their burdened heads,
Proudly laden with deep fragrance
In luscious shades of reds.

O were you only here with me
Their beauty to admire,
How greater far their loveliness
My dreaming would inspire.

January 12th, 1934

BROKEN INTERLUDE

DEARLY belovèd, it is thus we now end
Our hauntingly sweet interlude,
That to both of us with the promise of sorrow
And happiness rare was imbued?

It is thus we now end the gay comradeship
We held so blithely awhile,
With only a few lingering words of farewell,
The clasping of hands and a smile?

And will we remember the days that are gone
With something akin to regret,
Will the words that were spoken then haunt us,
Their memory paining us yet?

Will the knowledge of hours spent together
Seem sweeter the longer they're past,
And the thought of the other's loved face
Bring tears to our eyes at the last?

January 13th, 1934

SEA BLUE

THE sea is blue, a blue so deep
It reaches to my heart,
As I look upon its beauty
Tears to my eyelids start.

The sky above is a paler blue
And soft with silver clouds,
That float above the burning sea
In friendly little crowds.

But the sea is wildly blue and
Deep with eager laughter,
Flinging its spray like swords ahead
While the waves come swiftly after.

So I know I must have felt
That day when leaving you,
My pain was deep, deep as the sea,
And wild as the sea is blue.

January 13th, 1934

BROKEN DREAMING

To whom I loved I can never forget,
Though you be colder than starlight, and yet
It would be wiser perhaps to recall
That you never seemed to love me at all.

How when I offered my heart as a lute,
You remained indifferently mute
To its music, and turning your head
Spoke lightly with words brittle and dead.

Why have you felt the need to shatter
My dreaming; it would hardly matter
That I took one little dream away
To gladden my life each lonely day.

Why have you felt the need at the last
When all that was between us is past,
To embitter all my loneliness
With knowledge of your forgetfulness?

January 17th, 1934

HONOLULU

WHAT is this greenness
That lies in the sea,
Like and unknown theme
Of melody?

Where flowers cover
Both houses and trees,
In coloured clamour
Of harmonies.

Where waves reach slowly
With sapphire stretched hands,
To clasp the coveted
Gold of the sands.

Where the moon at night
Like silver raining,
Floods the island
With tender complaining.

Where Hawaiian songs
From plaintive guitars,
Fills our dreaming with
The light of stars.

What is this beauty
Never felt before,
That lies in the first
Sight of this shore?

January 17th, 1934

75

ROME

THE beauty of Rome lies like a flame
At my heart, indefinably dear;
Where cypress trees like sentinels
Dark against the evening sky, rear
Their noble heads in watchful quiet.

It was thus I saw them last along
The Appian Way, tall and sedate,
The proud guardians of lost glory;
that standing calmly seemed to wait
In peace, the end of all our worldly days.

Is sunset still a sacred thing in Rome?
And stretches the Campagna eagerly
In boundless beauty like a blessing
Toward the blue and distant sea,
In tender plea of loveliness?

And lingers holy quiet still
About the warm and sleeping city?
And do the prideful patient buildings
Move your heart with humble pity
For all that once was Rome, and is no more?

January 18th, 1934

DUSK IN BALI

DUSK falls soft on waters
Of terraced paddy fields,
That to the light of stars
Their mirrored surface yields.

The water buffalo
Returning from their toil,
Plod slowly through the damp
And sweet-smelling soil.

Down dusky village lanes
The evening fires are lit,
Where soft-voiced Balinese
Grouped dim in doorways sit.

Under a banyan tree
Slim girls are swayed in dance,
Beneath each flowered headdress
Their dark eyes dart and glance.

They glide in golden grace
To the gamelan bells,
Hands like fluttering petals
As the cool music swells.

Madé walks with Sampé
Pale blossoms in her hair:
Madé smiles into his eyes
Content to find him fair.

And all the while the scent
Of frangi-pani flowers,
Falls like a balm upon
The dark and tender hours.

January 18*th*, 1934

STAR DUST

Do inanimate things
Have memory,
Such as silver spoons
Or tapestry?

Do they remember that
His voice once fell,
Upon their ears like
A golden bell?

Do they know his glances
Like dust of stars,
Have lain upon them
For nameless hours?

Do they realize the
Touch of his hands,
Has given them life
Of sun-warmed sands?

Do they feel his moving
Among them yet
Has made the room like
A starlit net?

Or is it alone in
My heart I know,
He dwelt with these things
An hour or so?

January 21st, 1934

79

ROAD TO FEZ

THE smell of earth after rain
Is a very lovely thing,
Cool and fresh with fragrances
That seem sweet and promising.

Yet the smell of dust that lies
Here in the pitiless sun,
Has wrung my heart with a strange
Overwhelming compassion.

January 23rd, 1934

THE ENCHANTED

I HAVE known Enchantment,
Lain within her arms and heard her sigh;
Her voice has been my voice;
And in her smile I have seen the days go by.

We have gone hand in hand together
Through twilit streets at the hush of eve;
Have paused on curving bridges and heard
Far below the shadowed waters gently grieve.

We have wandered across the glory
Of San Marco's aflame with dying day;
Have lingered at night in the Grand Canal,
On whose surface the moon like a naiad lay.

Morn was to us a laughing child;
In dusk we have known a wistful friend;
Night has been our lover, and from his lips
We heard songs without beginning, without end.

I have known Enchantment,
Looked upon her face and seen her eyes;
It was at Venice that I found her, and there
She waits me still under gold-hung skies.

March 14th, 1934

RAVELLO

I WILL return one day to Ravello
And climb as of old the worn stone stair,
Till I reach the shade of a narrow street
Where the walls on both sides rise tall and bare.

I will stand as before in a garden
Covered with honeysuckle and roses,
And gaze at the valley below me
That the height of Ravello discloses.

The sea will lie away to the right
Softly blue ike the sigh of a dream;
And twilight with tender footsteps will dance
Across the sky in a glory of green.

Then beauty will ache deep in my heart
And tears of wonder will fill my eyes,
Love will flood my soul till my lips seem
To kiss the hair of the evening skies.

Once you were with me in Ravello
And together we watched the falling night,
You had placed a rose behind your ear
And smiled at me in the fading light.

I remember you sang as we strolled
Down the narrow and cobble-stoned street;
The stars were then shining above us
And their faces seemed tauntingly sweet.

When one day I return to Ravello
To find you are not there, will I recall
How the sunlight lay golden in pools
On the sheen of you smooth raven hair?

It can hardly have been because of you
That all these years I have loved it so,
Surely by then I will have forgotten
It was here that we came so long, long ago.

March 15th, 1934

NAPLES FROM PAOLO'S HOUSE

'GIVE me your hand
And let us stand
By the window here,
Now the sky is clear
With sunset, Barbara.

'Look, how Naples lies
At our feet, her eyes
Limpid with dreaming
All white and gleaming
With beauty, Barbara.

'Is she not tender
With patient surrender,
As evening closes
Like crimson roses
Above her head, Barbara?

'Hear the people singing
Down in the street, flinging
With each golden note
Their peasant souls afloat
In the air, Barbara.

'See, how the ocean
In darkening emotion
Lies stretched at her side,
In magnificent pride
Of Naples, Barbara.

'Have you ever seen
Ecstasy so clean
As this?' Paulo said,
With tears unshed
Filling his eyes.

I looked, and looking felt
My very heart must melt
At such stark beauty,
That was burdening me
So unutterably.

It was too great for bearing,
Too vast for sharing,
And knowing this I sighed;
Then suddenly I cried,
And turned my head aside.

January 22nd, 1934

TO VENICE

O VENICE, how the poor heart longs for you!
Each weary day that I rise anew
I sigh for you; and each sleepless night
My eyes are filled with your mellow light.

You alone are all my dreaming, and yet
I am disappointed; for in my mind's eye
I forever see your haunting face
Turned exquisitely toward the sky;

Till I myself became the sky, yearning
In ecstatic blue above your head;
I am the lover with outstretched arms,
And you the bride that I long to wed.

Yet alas! no marriage can ever be
No blending of earth and worshipful sky
For the whole of eternity between
Me and my beautiful love doth lie.

March 15th, 1934

MOONLIGHT IN GRANADA

IT was a minute Arab court
That lay before my eyes,
Whose simple white-washed walls
Were open to the skies.

It was bathed in shafts of moonlight
Thick as silver honey,
That fell upon my upturned palms
With the weight of silver money.

The stars in great profusion shone
Immensely large above,
And seemed to cleave the midnight blue
Like the winging of silver dove.

For this was the Alhambra where
The ghosts of Moors abide:
Within those silent chambers you
Can feel them by your side.

Before the little Arab court
I stood as in a trance
For against the moonlit wall did not
An Arab maiden dance?

March 18*th*, 1934

TREES

PINE trees upon a mountain side
Rearing great heads in lofty pride
Defy with scorn the heaven's blue
With outspread arms of sombre hue.

Beneath their mighty boughs of green
The light of day is dimly seen,
And there the air is cool with scent
That lulls the mind to sweet content.

Pine trees are the Nordsmen fierce and bold
Upon whose brows the clouds unfold,
Theirs is the earth to guard and keep
While mortal men are lost in sleep.

Slender palms that grow by the sea
And wave their branches gracefully
In plumes of green against the skies
Sway together with whispered sighs.

At night they lean towards the moon
And the wind like a plaintive tune
Sings to them words of soft endearing
That linger sweetly in their hearing.

Palm trees are dancers veiled and slight
With golden feet, that in the light
Of tropic day will dance a measure
To flood the traveller's heart with pleasure.

Cypress trees standing tall and straight
Beneath the dusk as though they wait
The ending of eternity
Have still remote majesty.

There is holiness that lingers
Like the touch of ghostly fingers
About their magnificent face
With an indescribable grace.

For cypress trees are memories
Of ancient Roman centuries,
Calm with the stupendous glory
Of their eternal story.

March 5th, 1934

SUNSET AT THE SUMMER PALACE

IT was sunset, and the light shone
Tenderly like a caress;
The western hills wore a brooding
Mantle of happiness.

We stood high upon a terrace
Close to the evening sky;
The lake to the south dreamily
Lay watching the daylight die.

Below us curving palace roofs
Were covered with tiles of gold,
That proudly stood as though waiting
With faces majestically old.

Against the eastern horizon
Peking lay like a shade of night;
The western hills were purple giants
That had hidden the sun from sight.

And I felt that Death was everywhere,
Over palaces, hills, and lake;
The courtyards were thronged with spirits
That the coming of night seemed to wake.

March 17th, 1934

IN A PEKING STREET

HAVE you ever ridden
Through a dusty Peking street,
Past brown-faced women
Who walk on binded feet?

Past shops with painted lanterns
Laden with curios,
And carts where bright persimmons
Are ranged in orange rows?

Have you ever listened
To the noise of such a street,
Where beggered blind musicians
Play music wildly sweet?

Where shrill-voiced, blue-clad vendors
Extol their varied wares,
With the aid of camel bells
And confidential airs?

Have you ever marvelled at
The joy on Chinese faces,
And the ease of dignity
Their slightest move embraces?

At the cheerful disorder
Of grace and confusion,
Where coolies and princes mix
In nameless profusion?

Have you loved the sight
Of rickshaws speeding by,
Beneath the brilliant sun
Of a blue and cloudless sky?

Where long-robed Chinese merchants
Recline with folded arms,
Indifferent to the scene
Of Peking's dusty charms?

April 18*th*, 1934

RENCONTRE

I OFTEN dream how the cool tones
Of your voice will fall like rain
On the parched desert of my heart,
When first meeting with you again.

I recall that they ring like bells
With a rich and sudden laughter,
Baring my heart like a darkened hill
In the calm that follows after.

Your eyes will be blue as savage
Stars that blaze in a tropic night,
And your glance will be swift as a
Flock of swallows in homing flight.

Your skin was ever a lovely
Thing like ambrosia of morn,
And your hair was the darkened gold
Of an approaching summer dawn.

There was a peculiar grace in
The lithe manner of your moving,
That was at once tantalising
And yet altogether soothing.

I remember the words you spoke
Were clear and meaningless as air,
While your eyes seemed a challenge of
Flame taunting me to despair.

I dream of meeting you again
Tho' my dreams are clouded with fear;
What if I find you have become
An unknown stranger standing near?

March 26th, 1934

PRAYER FOR LIGHT

O LORD, would you take the stars from the sky
To leave it a dim unlovely thing?
Would the thought of those wide unseeing eyes
Not cause you to grieve at such suffering?

Would you steal the sun from a summer day
As it nourished the hungry earth with light?
Would you plunge it without compassion
Into a darkened void of endless night?

Would you banish the blue of the ocean
And the fragrance of flowers in spring,
Would you silence the voice of nightingales
And not weep for the songs that they would sing?

O Lord, in your mercy heed my prayer
And stay your hand from the eyes of night,
Take not the world's birthright of beauty
But restore to the good the boon of sight.

April 7th, 1934

LAST NIGHT

LAST night when close to you
  I would have cried,
But my tears were hidden
  Deep inside.

How great is grief when held
  Within your breast.
For often only tears
  Can give you rest.

April 29th, 1934

96

TO —

WHEN I look upon your face,
Beside me fresh and clear,
I marvel that God made you
So exquisitely dear.

Or when I watch you moving
With movements lithe and free,
I know the love I bear you
Is overwhelming me.

And when I hear you speak my name
In a voice so rich and sweet,
I feel the stars of heaven
Are fallen at my feet.

April 29th, 1934

PATTERNS

THE other day you said
You were not for me,
That our love was a dream
Never meant to be.

And I heard you with tears
That flooded my eyes,
To think you could tell me
Such terrible lies.

For in my heart I knew
What you failed to see,
That God had created
You only for me.

As a hill that holds grass
Green-grown to her breast;
As trees thick with foliage
That brings the earth rest;

As streams that run clearly
Through meadows and field;
As stars in the evening
Their brilliances yield;

As all these are patterns
Of eternity,
So I know in my soul
You are meant for me.

May 12th, 1934

98

A PLAINT

I WOULD have given you my heart
As a road of roses for your feet,
I thought perhaps my love for you
Might make your life complete.

I would have given you my life
Although the gift be poor indeed,
Yet now I know of both these things,
Alas! you have no need.

May 6th, 1934

THIS SPRING IN PARIS

NOW you are gone life is
Weariness without ending,
I move more vainly through the days
My mind uncomprehending.

I am told the chestnut trees
Have blossomed once again,
And lilac bushes in the Bois
Rise thick as mists of rain.

That all along the Seine
The air is soft with spring,
And in the grass-grown borders
The morning skylarks sing.

That hidden in green leaves there
Are strawberries to find,
That the sky is smiling blue
And clouds are silver lined.

But what is this to me
Now you are gone away?
For not all the loveliness
Of spring could make you stay.

May 7th, 1934

A SHADOW

WE were together in this room
One night not long ago,
There is the couch on which we sat
And loved each other so.

Though hardly a word was spoken
And scarce you touched my hand,
For hearts need no declaration
Of love to understand.

But to-night there are others here
With voices light and gay,
Who know not that I am alone
Now you have gone away.

How strange that this room should remain
Exactly as before,
Save, for me, where once you stood, lies
A shadow on the floor.

May 10*th*, 1934

ADIEU

I WILL not grieve
Though we may part,
For you have become
The whole of my heart.

The sun never mourns
For days that are fled,
For deep in her soul
Their beauty is bred.

The earth never weeps
For trees that are felled,
For deep in her breast
Their spirits are held.

The sky never sighs
For a starless night,
For deep in her eyes
Is burning their light.

So how can I grieve
When we have become
Like stars and the sky,
Like days and the sun?

Therefore, adieu,
My dearest heart,
For nevermore
Will we be apart.

April 28th, 1934

www.ingramcontent.com/pod-product-compliance
Lightning Source LLC
Chambersburg PA
CBHW030640150426
42811CB00076B/1970/J